BUILT NOT BORN

Do What's Right™
The 7 Shifts to Scale Your Business
Lead with Integrity, and Win in Life

Larry G. Dix II

Built Not Born: Do What's Right™:
The 7 Shifts to Scale Your Business, Lead with Integrity, and Win in Life

ISBN: 979-8-9931917-2-0 (Paperback)
ISBN: 979-8-9931917-3-7 (HardCover)
ISBN: 979-8-9931917-5-1 (EBook)
Library of Congress Control Number: 2026908276

Published by Plot Twist Ink

www.PlotTwistInk.com

Do What's Right™ is a registered trademark of Larry G. Dix II.

Co-authored by Larry G. Dix II and Bridgetta Tomarchio
Written and developed in collaboration with Bridgetta Tomarchio, Plot Twist Ink

Scripture quotations are taken from the Holy Bible, New International Version®, NIV®. Copyright © 1973, 1978, 1984, 2011 by Biblica, Inc.™ Used by permission. All rights reserved worldwide.

Cover design by Bridgetta Tomarchio
Cover and author photography by TaylorAnn Tallman of Lil Bug Photos

Printed in the United States of America.
First Edition: 2026

DEDICATION

To my family,
For your love, your patience, and your belief in me
through every season of building.

And to God,
For the strength, the correction, and the grace that
made this journey possible.

To those who choose to do what is right,
even when it costs you. You are the ones building
something that lasts.

TABLE OF CONTENTS

INTRODUCTION

I didn't just set out to write any book. I set out to change my life. Not because everything around me was falling apart, but because I knew something within me needed to change. On the outside, I had built businesses, carried responsibility, and experienced a level of success that many people spend their lives chasing. But internally, there were areas where I lacked consistency, discipline, and alignment. There were gaps between what I said I valued and how I was actually living.

That kind of misalignment is easy to ignore for a while. You can stay busy. You can achieve results. You can convince yourself that things are working. But eventually, you begin to recognize that success without structure is unstable. You begin to feel the weight of inconsistency. You begin to see that winning in one area does not make up for a lack of integrity in another.

That realization forced me to confront a truth that applies to every one of us: no one is coming to fix your life for you. No one is coming to create your discipline, to align your habits, or to raise your standards. If anything is going to change, it begins with a decision you make and a commitment you choose to keep.

For me, everything started there, not with motivation or inspiration, but with a decision. A decision to stop negotiating with myself. A decision to stop waiting for the right time or the right feeling. A decision to take ownership of how I was living and who I was becoming.

That single decision led to a series of shifts that did more than improve my results. They reshaped my identity. They changed how I approached my time, my habits, my leadership, my health, and my faith. Over time, those shifts became a framework I could rely on, not just when things were going well, but especially when they were not.

I call them the 7 Shifts.

They are not complicated, but they are foundational. They are the difference between living reactively and living intentionally. They are the difference between starting strong and finishing strong. Most people do not struggle because they lack information. They struggle because they lack structure. These shifts provide that structure.

They begin with deciding before you feel ready, because waiting for readiness will keep you stuck. They continue with letting go of motivation and building discipline, because feelings will never sustain what your life requires. They move into creating routines that anchor your day, cutting what does not serve you, and fueling your body and mind so you can operate with clarity and strength. From there, they lead into building your leadership from the inside out, and finally, into delivering consistently, every single day, in every area that matters.

Each shift builds on the one before it. Together, they form a standard.

This book is not about becoming perfect. It is about becoming aligned. It is about closing the gap between your words and your actions. It is about becoming the kind of person who follows through, regardless of how you feel in the moment.

That kind of alignment changes everything. It builds confidence, not from outcomes, but from evidence. When you consistently keep your word to yourself, you no longer question who you are. You know.

That is where real leadership begins.

As you move through this book, you will notice that it is not designed to simply be read. It is designed to be used. Each chapter includes a workbook section, not as an add-on, but as an essential part of the process. Reading without application creates awareness. Application creates transformation. If you are willing to engage with what you are reading, to write things down, to take action, and to reflect honestly, you will begin to see change happen in real time.

If you are not, nothing will change.

Growth does not come from consuming more information. It comes from doing something with what you already know.

Throughout this book, one principle will continue to surface: Do What's Right™.

Not what is easy. Not what is comfortable. Not what is convenient. What is right.

That principle has guided me through some of the most difficult decisions I have faced. It has required me to choose long-term integrity over short-term gain, to take responsibility when it would have been easier to deflect, and to act with discipline when I did not feel like it. It has not always been the easiest path, but it has always been the right one. And over time, it has proven to be the most rewarding one.

Because what you do repeatedly shapes who you become.

Every decision you make is building something. Every action you take is reinforcing an identity. You are either building discipline or weakening it. You are either strengthening your standards or lowering them. You are either becoming more aligned or more divided.

There is no neutral.

This book is about helping you take control of that process. It is about moving from inconsistency to discipline, from reaction to intention, and from uncertainty to clarity. It is about becoming someone who does not wait to feel ready, but decides and moves forward anyway.

You do not need to be born with that kind of discipline or clarity.

You build it.

One decision at a time.
One discipline at a time.
One day at a time.

And that is how it's formed. Built Not Born.

BUILT NOT BORN

Chapter 1
Decide Before You're Ready

*"Commit to the Lord whatever you do, and he will
establish your plans."*
~Proverbs 16:3 (NIV)~

I wasn't ready. I did not feel inspired. I did not wake
up one morning overflowing with confidence, clarity,
and courage. There was no moment where everything
lined up and gave me permission to begin. I simply
made a decision anyway.

That's the truth about real change. It rarely arrives
when life feels calm, clean, and convenient. It does
not wait for your schedule to open up or for January
1st to come. It does not wait until the fear disappears.
It does not wait until you feel fully qualified. It begins
when you decide, even while uncertainty is still
present and doubt is still speaking. Real change
begins in a moment of decision, when you draw a line
in the sand and say, this is over, this is who I am now,
and this is how I move forward.

Most people spend their lives waiting for a feeling that was never meant to lead them. They wait for the perfect Monday. They wait for the perfect new year. They wait until business slows down. They wait until the kids get older. They wait until their stress goes away. They wait until they feel brave. Waiting often disguises fear in a way that feels responsible or justified.

What looks like patience is often hesitation. What feels like preparation is often avoidance. In business, this shows up as over planning, over analyzing, and delaying execution under the illusion of being responsible. A decision cuts through all of that noise.

Motivation is different. It is emotional. It is unpredictable. It comes and goes. Some days it shows up. Some days it disappears. Some days it is strong in the morning and gone by lunch. If your life is built on motivation, then your consistency will always rise and fall with your feelings.

Motivation asks, *"Do I feel like it today?"*

Decision says, *"This is who I am now, whether I feel like it or not."*

As leadership expert John Maxwell puts it, *"Motivation gets you going, but discipline keeps you growing."* That truth matters because too many people are trying to build a disciplined life on an emotional foundation. It cannot hold. Feelings are unstable. Identity is stable. And for entrepreneurs, this distinction is critical, because your business will demand consistency long after your emotions have checked out.

When you make a real decision, you stop asking for permission from your emotions. You stop checking in with comfort before you act. You stop consulting fear as if it has wisdom to offer. You remove the need to renegotiate with yourself every single day. You eliminate the internal boardroom meeting that most people hold every morning before they take action. You simply make a move.

That is why a true decision is so powerful. It simplifies life. It creates clarity. It removes the friction that keeps most people stuck.

And science backs this up. Researchers who study willpower and behavior have found that the human brain only has so much energy for repeated choices. The more often you force yourself to revisit the same question, the more drained you become. Every internal debate takes energy. Every maybe consumes strength. Every small act of hesitation chips away at momentum. But when a decision becomes firm, your mind no longer has to keep circling the issue. You conserve energy because the debate is over. You are no longer spending mental energy deciding, only executing.

You no longer ask, *"Should I do this today? Should I keep going? Is this the right time?"* You already decided. You removed the question before the day even began.

That is what creates freedom. Not the absence of responsibility, but the removal of internal conflict.

I experienced this truth firsthand when it came to drinking. For years, I tried to manage it instead of ending it. I told myself I would cut back. I told myself I would slow down when the timing was better. I told myself I would deal with it later. The problem was not that alcohol controlled every area of my life. The problem was that deep down, I knew it did not belong in the future I wanted to build. It was a distraction. It was noise. It was one more thing taking up space in a life that needed greater clarity.

Then one day, I was recording a podcast with a friend. He told me he had been sober for seventeen years. Hearing that landed deep in me. It did not feel like casual conversation. It felt like conviction. It was a moment of clarity that demanded a response. It forced me to confront something I had been avoiding for a long time. In that moment, it was as if God spoke directly to my spirit and said, *"You will never drink again."*

That was it. The decision was immediate and final. No tapering off, or "maybe next month." From that day forward, I was done.

What made that moment powerful was not the plan. It was the finality of the decision. I did not leave the door cracked open. I shut it. I did not say I was trying. I said I was done. That difference matters.

The first week, the thought of drinking still crossed my mind. But the relief was stronger than the craving. Each day I said no, I felt lighter as I reinforced the identity I had chosen. Each time I followed through, I was proving to myself that I was no longer the person who negotiated with that habit.

I learned something in that season that applies to every area of life. Once a decision is made at the identity level, you do not have to fight the same battle every day. You remove it. You end the negotiation.

That was a major shift for me. What had weighed on me for years was suddenly gone. Not because temptation vanished overnight, but because indecision vanished overnight. The internal war had ended.

And that one decision became the first domino. Once I proved I could do that, I started proving I could do more. That is when I began to understand how much power a true decision carries, and it marked the beginning of a completely different direction for my life.

That is how transformation often begins. It begins with one act of finality. One clear choice. One honest moment where you stop playing games with yourself. One moment where you stop saying someday and start saying now.

Most people assume discipline comes after motivation. *"Once I feel like it, then I'll start."* But the reality is the opposite. You don't wait for discipline to show up; you build it through decisions that stick.

Discipline is not magic. It is not a personality trait reserved for the gifted or the intense. It is the result of repeated obedience to a decision you already made. It is built through daily follow through, especially on the days when there is no emotion supporting you and no external pressure forcing you to act.

That's what happened with my mornings. For most of my life, I woke up when I had to. I wasn't lazy, but I wasn't intentional either. Then, in June of 2025, I decided to start waking up at 5 AM.

The first week was easier than expected. Novelty will do that. It gives you a short burst of motivation. But by the second week, the excitement faded. The bed felt warmer, the alarm felt louder, and the excuses started creeping in.

That is always the test. The beginning is rarely the hardest part. The hardest part is what comes after the beginning, when the emotion wears off and the commitment is all that remains. That is where identity is either reinforced or abandoned.

That's when I created a simple ritual: the second my feet hit the ground, I bow my head and pray. I thank God for another day and ask Him for focus. That prayer turned what could have been a struggle into an anchor. Over time, 5 AM became 4 AM. And once again, the decision was final.

That prayer did more than give me a quiet moment. It placed my mind in the right order. Before the phone, the demands, the noise, and the pressure. Before anyone needed anything from me, I remembered who gave me breath in the first place. I remembered who I answer to. I remembered that the day belongs to God before it belongs to me.

Here's the payoff: by the time most people are pouring their first cup of coffee, I've already been awake for hours. I've prayed, trained, read, and worked. My body is sharp, my mind is focused, and my spirit is aligned before the world can throw its chaos at me. When I walk into a meeting or a challenge, I carry the confidence of someone who has already won the day.

That kind of confidence is different from ego. It is not loud. It is not performative. It is not rooted in pride. It is quiet confidence, the kind that comes from keeping promises to yourself. It comes from knowing you have already followed through before the day even begins.

Small kept promises become personal evidence. And evidence changes identity. Over time, that identity becomes something you no longer question.

A motivated person may begin. A decided person continues. And in business, continuation is what separates those who build from those who stall.

Research shows that when you make a clear, firm decision, your brain actually reorganizes itself to conserve energy. Psychologists call it "decision closure." Instead of fighting with yourself every day, *"Should I? Shouldn't I?"* you've already closed the door. The debate is over. That's why decision is so much stronger than motivation: it frees up your energy to act.

This is one of the reasons so many people feel mentally exhausted before they have done anything meaningful. It is not always because they are working too hard. Sometimes it is because they are negotiating too often. They are asking themselves the same questions every morning. Will I do it today. Will I stay committed. Will I give in. Will I start over Monday. They are restarting the same internal conversation instead of executing a decision that has already been made. That constant mental churn drains the soul.

A clear decision creates peace because it removes the argument. It removes the constant negotiation that drains your focus and weakens your follow through.

Waking up early was never really about the clock. It was about ownership. It was about proving that I was capable of leading myself before trying to lead anyone else. It was about refusing to let comfort make decisions for me. Each time I kept that commitment, I was proving something to myself: *I'm not the kind of man who negotiates with comfort. I'm the kind of man who does what he says.*

That is integrity. Integrity is not about being perfect. It is about alignment. When your words and your actions match, you build trust, first with yourself, and then with everyone who is watching.

And this matters more than most people realize. Self trust is the root of all strong leadership. If you cannot trust yourself to follow through, then deep down you will hesitate in business, in relationships, in faith, and in pressure. But when you become a man or woman who honors your own commitments, something powerful happens. Your voice gains weight. Your standards rise, and your decisions become cleaner.

That is the real secret of discipline. Every time you make a decision and back it up with action, you stack another layer onto your identity. One decision builds on the next. That is how momentum grows, not in giant leaps, but in small, repeated wins.

Success rarely looks dramatic while you are building it. Most of the time, it looks ordinary. It looks like getting up when you said you would. It looks like saying no when no one would have known if you said yes. It looks like training when you feel tired. It looks like praying when you feel dry. It looks like doing the next right thing, over and over again, until your life becomes the evidence of your values.

That's exactly what happened with my workouts.

Discipline isn't built on feelings. It's built on repeated follow-through.

Motivation says, *"I'll work out when I feel like it."*

Decision says, *"I train because that's who I am."*

For years, I thought I had discipline, but what I really had was bursts of motivation. I would dabble in different types of workouts, run a marathon here, try CrossFit there, cycle across Florida, and then move on. I would check the box, but I never stuck with anything long enough to create lasting change. The problem was not effort. It was decision.

That is an important distinction. Effort without identity creates inconsistency. You can work hard for a while and still never change if you do not decide who you are. Activity alone does not transform you. Repeated alignment does.

That moment came in October of 2023. I was visiting family in Texas when my mother-in-law looked me straight in the eye and said, *"You're getting fat."*

It stung, but she was right. I had let myself slide. That was the wake up call. The first week was not glamorous. There were no breakthroughs, no instant results to keep me going, just tons of sweat and soreness that reminded me how far I had drifted and the same voice in my head telling me to skip a day. But I didn't. I had already made the decision, and once I do that, there is no going back.

That first stretch matters because it is where identity gets forged. Not when the compliments come. Not when the scale changes. Not when the outside world notices. Identity gets forged in the private repetitions that nobody applauds.

To make it non-negotiable, I tied my workouts into my morning foundation. I wake up at 4 AM, and training is the very first thing I do. No debates. No excuses. Just move my body, every single day. Over time, it became an identity. Since October 2023, I haven't missed a single day.

It is not about vanity. It is about integrity. It is about being the man who does what he says. That integrity spills into every area of my life, whether it is my leadership, my business, or my family. My employees know I will do whatever it takes to protect their jobs. My bankers know I will fight to make payroll, even if it means I go without. And my grandchildren will grow up knowing their grandfather is disciplined, not because I talk about it, but because I live it.

That is the deeper point. Discipline is never isolated. It always spills over. The man who keeps his word in private becomes more trustworthy in public. The leader who learns to master comfort becomes steadier under pressure. The entrepreneur who honors his own commitments becomes more dependable in the eyes of clients, employees, lenders, partners, and family.

Motivation never got me here. Decision did. And once I made that choice, discipline carried it forward.

Henry Ford famously said, *"Whether you think you can, or you think you can't, you're right."*

I believe there is something deeper underneath that idea. What you repeatedly decide about yourself becomes the life you start living. If you decide you are the kind of person who quits when it gets hard, you will keep proving that true. If you decide you are the kind of person who follows through, you will start building evidence for that too.

Jim Rohn said, *"Discipline is the bridge between goals and accomplishment."*

I have found that to be true in every serious area of life. Goals are easy to write down. Vision is easy to talk about. But discipline is the first plank in that bridge. And in business, this matters even more.

Entrepreneurs do not have the luxury of living by emotion. Their responsibilities do not pause when motivation disappears. A company cannot be built on moods. Payroll cannot be met by inspiration alone. Teams do not need a leader who feels like showing up. They need a leader who has already decided what kind of person he is going to be when things get hard.

That is why I believe one of the most dangerous lies in personal growth is this idea that you need to feel ready before you begin. Readiness is overrated. In many cases, readiness never comes. You become ready by moving. You become clearer by acting. You become stronger by carrying weight. You become disciplined by doing disciplined things before they feel natural.

Nobody becomes courageous before they act courageously. Nobody becomes focused before they practice focus. Nobody becomes consistent before they choose consistency while it is still uncomfortable.

As we wrap this first shift, let me leave you with something to anchor in, the deeper reason *decision* matters more than motivation.

> *"Every time you decide once and remove the debate, you conserve energy for action. Decision frees the brain. Motivation drains it."*

Our brains are wired for efficiency. Every day, we make hundreds, even thousands, of small choices, what to eat, whether to get up, what to check first, what to avoid, what to delay. Each of those choices consumes mental energy. Psychology and neuroscience show that willpower is a limited resource, and when you force yourself to re decide over and over, you burn through it. But when you make a firm decision up front, it conserves mental bandwidth. The debate is closed. You eliminate the internal tug of war.

That is why the strongest people are often the simplest people. They simplify what has already been decided. They remove needless choice from areas where conviction already exists. They do not wake up each morning and renegotiate their values.

You see, when you decide, your brain begins to align with that choice. Your thoughts become cleaner. Your attention becomes less fragmented. Your actions become more direct. You shift from asking, should I do this, to declaring, this is what I do.

Decision removes the need to feel ready and replaces it with action. Motivation flickers. It depends on mood, energy, and external circumstances. Decision is structural. It becomes your identity. Each major shift you commit to, quitting, waking early, training, praying first, doing what is right even when it costs you, adds another layer to who you become.

When you decide in advance, you trade chaos for structure. You remove internal friction and create forward momentum. That is the foundation of what it means to become Built Not Born.

You are not waiting to become someone else. You are deciding to become someone else.

And maybe that is where this chapter needs to land. Not on behavior alone, but on belief. You do not need more time before you start. You do not need a cleaner past. You do not need a different personality. You do not need ideal conditions. You need a decision. A true one. A final one. A decision that is rooted not in emotion, but in identity and conviction.

The life you want will not be built by wishing. It will be built through decisive action followed by consistent follow through. The discipline you admire will not appear by accident, it will be built through repetition over time. The confidence you crave will not be handed to you by success first. It will grow after you keep promises to yourself.

That is where everything changes. It begins with one decision that you refuse to revisit, a decision that closes the door on who you were and establishes a higher standard for who you are becoming. From there, it is built through consistent follow through, through showing up again and again, regardless of how you feel.

This is what separates those who stay average from those who rise above. This is how leaders are forged and how character is built over time. Not through intensity alone, but through consistency. This is how you become Built Not Born.

****

Action Steps

"Motivation asks if you feel like it. Decision declares who you are."

Don't wait to feel ready. Don't wait for motivation. Decide now. Act now.

Try This:

- Choose one decision you've been avoiding.
- Commit to it today with no debate, no "maybe."
- Take one small action within the next twenty four hours.
- Do it for 7 days straight. No excuses.
- Track it. Journal it. Pay attention to what shifts.

Once you prove to yourself that you *can* decide and act, something powerful happens. The next decision becomes easier. Momentum builds. Identity begins to shift. You stop seeing yourself as someone who tries and start seeing yourself as someone who follows through.

Reinforce Your Life Code

Decision. Discipline. Determination. Deliver.

This is more than just a slogan, it's an operating system. Decision starts the chain. Discipline sustains it. Determination carries you through resistance. Deliver seals your reputation, with yourself and with others.

This is how trust is built. This is how confidence grows. This is how leaders separate themselves from those who continue to wait.

"Let your 'Yes' be 'Yes,' and your 'No,' 'No.' Anything beyond this comes from the evil one."

~Matthew 5:37 (NIV)~

~Chapter 1 Workbook~

Decide Before You're Ready

1. The Decision You've Been Avoiding

Write it clearly. No soft language. No hesitation.

2. Close the Door

What are you DONE negotiating with?

3. Identity Shift

I am the kind of person who:

____

____

I no longer:

____

____

I now operate as someone who:

____

____

4. Your First Action

What is the first action you will take within 24 hours?

____

____

Date: _____________ Time: _____________

5. 7 Day Commitment

What is your daily non negotiable action?

____

This is your 7 day proof. No skipping. No restarting. No excuses.

Check off each day after completion:

Day 1 ☐
Day 2 ☐
Day 3 ☐
Day 4 ☐
Day 5 ☐
Day 6 ☐
Day 7 ☐

Notice how your confidence shifts as you keep your word to yourself.

6. What Changed

What resistance came up?

____

____

What did you feel after following through?

____

____

What did you learn about yourself?

____

____

7. Your Life Code

Decision. Discipline. Determination. Deliver.

What does each mean to you?

Decision:

Discipline:

Determination:

Deliver:

"If anyone, then, knows the good they ought to do and doesn't do it, it is sin."

~James 4:17 (NIV)~

Chapter 2
Stop Chasing Motivation

"No discipline seems pleasant at the time, but painful. Later on, however, it produces a harvest of righteousness and peace for those who have been trained by it."

~Hebrews 12:11 (NIV)~

Chapter 1 was about the decision. This chapter is about what happens after the decision has been made. It is about what you do the next day, and the day after that, and the day after that. This is where most people fall apart, not in deciding, but in sustaining the decision when nothing feels exciting anymore.

Motivation is a mood. Discipline is what carries you when the mood disappears.

Hebrews 12:11 makes this clear. Discipline is not about enjoying the process, it is about the outcome it produces over time. Most people wait until they "feel motivated" to take action. They wait for the perfect mood, the perfect day, or the spark of inspiration. But by then, the moment has already passed. In business, this delay is costly. Opportunities do not wait for your mood to align.

Motivation feels powerful in the moment, but it has no staying power. It rises quickly and disappears just as fast. Discipline, on the other hand, is quiet, steady, and consistent. It does not need excitement to operate. It only needs commitment.

A decision may change your direction, but discipline determines your outcome. Anyone can decide once. Very few follow through daily. That is where the separation happens. This is where entrepreneurs either build momentum or lose it entirely.

Most people do not fail because they made the wrong decision. They fail because they stopped executing the right one. I learned this the hard way.

Motivation is unreliable. It's like the weather, it changes hour by hour, and you can't control it. If you only take action when you feel like it, you'll never be consistent. And without consistency, you'll never build momentum.

I have been there. In the late 1990s, I made the decision to finally run a marathon after years of talking about it. At first, I was fired up. I ran two marathons and countless races over the next few years. But once business started going well, I got complacent. I thought I had it all figured out. I quit running, lost momentum, and paid the price. Success without discipline will always lead to regression.

A buddy of mine introduced me to CrossFit, and I dove in again. Lost 40 pounds in six months. Felt great. But once more, I got complacent. By 2020, I was slower, heavier, and relying on daily pills for blood pressure and acid reflux. That was my wake up call. I realized motivation had carried me only so far, and when it ran out, I had nothing to lean on. That is the danger of building your life on something that cannot sustain you.

That pattern is more common than people realize. Motivation creates spikes. Discipline creates standards. Spikes feel exciting, but they do not last. Standards feel ordinary, but they change everything.

That is the truth most people do not want to face. Motivation can start a season, but it cannot sustain a life.

What I needed was structure, something that did not depend on how I felt that day. If you wait for motivation, you will always be behind.

"Feelings lie. Discipline tells the truth."

Motivation will tell you to stay in bed. Discipline gets you on your feet. Motivation will tell you comfort is enough. Discipline demands better.

Motivation is driven by emotion. Discipline is driven by standards. Motivation asks what you feel like doing. Discipline asks what you committed to doing.

Discipline is like a muscle. The more you use it, the stronger it gets. Every time you act when you do not feel like it, you strengthen your identity.

And this is where everything shifts. You are no longer deciding who you are. You are proving it through repetition. That strength carries into your body, your business, and your leadership. It becomes visible in how you show up under pressure, not just when things are easy.

For me, the cold plunge is the perfect reminder. I work out every day for over an hour, and yet I still wrestle with three minutes in freezing water. It plays mind games with me every time. Some mornings I stall, staring at the water, trying to psych myself up.

But I still get in, not because I want to, but because I made the commitment. It is never fun. The first thirty seconds are brutal. But once I am through, I know I have already conquered the hardest thing I will face that day. I have already proven that my actions are not controlled by my comfort.

That moment is not about motivation. It is about choice.

"Discipline is choosing between what you want now and what you want most."
~Abraham Lincoln~

Discipline is built in those moments, not once, but over and over again. That is what discipline does. It gives you evidence before the day even begins. It gives you proof that you can follow through regardless of how you feel.

When life comes at you with frustrations, traffic, delays, a client who cancels, a deal that falls apart, you are not as shaken.

Why? Because before the world even woke up, you already won a battle with yourself. You proved you can push through resistance. So the rest of the day feels lighter.

Most people get thrown off by the first inconvenience because they have built no resilience. But when you anchor your day in discipline, setbacks do not hit the same way. Instead of reacting, you are grounded in your responses. They do not control you, because you have already proven that you control your response.

Neuroscience explains why this works. Studies show that self control is like a muscle. When you exercise it in one area, you strengthen it in others. By doing something hard first thing in the morning, you activate your prefrontal cortex, the part of the brain responsible for focus, decision making, and emotional control. Discipline does not just strengthen your body, it strengthens your ability to stay steady under pressure.

Psychologists call this "preloading willpower." By proving to yourself early that you can follow through, you lower your stress response later in the day. Cortisol spikes less, patience lasts longer, and you're able to respond instead of react.

That's why something like a cold plunge or a workout isn't just fitness. It is preparation. It is training your mind to stay steady when everything around you is not. If you can master yourself in the morning, you can master your response to whatever the world throws at you.

This is exactly what Scripture teaches about perseverance.

"Consider it pure joy, my brothers and sisters, whenever you face trials of many kinds, because you know that the testing of your faith produces perseverance. Let perseverance finish its work so that you may be mature and complete, not lacking anything."

~ James 1:2–4 (NIV)~

When you choose discipline early, you build perseverance that carries you through the trials of the day. It's not just physical training, it's spiritual training. Discipline teaches you to endure. Endurance makes you mature. And maturity equips you to lead from a place of strength, not reaction.

Success is built on repeated follow through. Small wins stacked on top of each other until they become your identity.

Every time you keep a promise to yourself, you rewrite your identity. You stop being someone who tries. You become someone who delivers.

As Aristotle is often credited with saying, *"We are what we repeatedly do. Excellence, then, is not an act, but a habit."*

Psychology backs this up. Research in Harvard Business Review found that recognizing and recording small wins creates a progress loop. Each time you complete an action, your brain releases dopamine, not from comfort, but from accomplishment. Over time, you begin to crave discipline instead of distraction.

That is why I love stacking small wins. They create momentum. One win turns into two, then ten, then a hundred. Before long, discipline is no longer something you force. It becomes something you are.

That's why I never wait for dates. I don't wait until Monday, or January 1st, or my birthday to start. I start now. I build momentum now. I act. Then I repeat. Then I reinforce. That is the cycle that builds discipline.

Discipline is not just about workouts. Reading your Bible daily is discipline. Praying daily is discipline. Eating well is discipline. Learning something new every day is discipline.

Your habits are not random. They are rehearsals for your future. They are patterns that will either build your life or slowly work against it. Habits are muscles. The question is: are you building positive ones or negative ones?

****

Action Steps:

Break Free from Motivation

"Motivation gets you started. Discipline gets you finished."

Don't wait for motivation. Don't wait to feel ready. Start now.

- Pick one thing you've been avoiding.
- Commit to it daily for the next 7 days.
- Don't measure how you feel. Measure what you do.
- Track your follow-through, not your feelings.
- At the end of 7 days, notice how your confidence has shifted.

Confidence is not built by thinking. It is built by follow-through.

Prove to yourself you can act without waiting for motivation. Once you do, you'll never go back. The leaders who last aren't the ones who wait for inspiration; they're the ones who act on principle.

That's why this shift matters: Stop chasing motivation. Start building discipline.

Decision. Discipline. Determination. Deliver.

"Like a city whose walls are broken through is a person who lacks self-control."

~Proverbs 25:28~

Paul compares discipline to training as an athlete; it's about controlling the body, not letting it control you. It is about leading yourself instead of reacting to your impulses. That's the essence of this shift: discipline is what carries you forward when motivation runs out.

Discipline is not a feeling. It is a standard you live by. It is the structure that supports every decision you have already made.

But here's the key: even discipline needs a place to live. If you want to make discipline last, you have to anchor it in a structure that grounds you every single day. That anchor is your routine. And that's where we go next.

~Chapter 2 Workbook~

Execute Without Emotion

**You are not deciding anymore.
You are proving it through action.**

1. Your One Non Negotiable Action

What is the ONE action you will complete every day for the next 7 days? Make it measurable. Make it repeatable. Make it undeniable. This must be clear and repeatable.

____

____

____

2. Define the Standard

What counts as "done"? Be specific so there is no debate or excuse. If it is not defined, it will be negotiated.

For example, Don't just write "work out." Be specific. Write what you will do like: "Lift weights for 30 minutes minimum, no phone, no interruptions, full focus."

3. Set the Time

When will this happen daily?

Time:

What triggers it? Attach it to something that already happens so there is no decision required.

4. Track Execution Only

Do not track feelings. Do not track effort. Track one thing only: Did you do it?

Check off ONLY if completed:

Day 1 ☐
Day 2 ☐
Day 3 ☐
Day 4 ☐
Day 5 ☐
Day 6 ☐
Day 7 ☐

No check mark means it did not happen.

5. Missed Day Rule

If you miss a day, what is your correction? Decide this now so there is no negotiation later. Missed days are not failures. They are tests of your standard.

6. Results

At the end of 7 days:

Did you complete all 7 days?

YES ☐ NO ☐

If no, how many days did you complete? _______

7. Proof

Complete this sentence based on your ACTIONS, not intentions:

This week proved that I am someone who:

____

____

____

____

8. Next Move

Will you continue this for another 7 days?

YES ☐ NO ☐

If yes, what is the next level of this action? Raise the standard or repeat it until it becomes automatic.

Discipline is not built in one moment. It is built in repetition. You do not become disciplined by deciding. You become disciplined by doing it again tomorrow. And then doing it again the next day. And the next. Until it becomes who you are.

"I have fought the good fight, I have finished the race, I have kept the faith.

~2 Timothy 4:7 (NIV)~

Discipline is built in the small things. And the small things are what build everything.

Chapter 3
Your Routine is Your Foundation

"Very early in the morning, while it was still dark, Jesus got up, left the house and went off to a solitary place, where he prayed."

~Mark 1:35 (NIV)~

Jesus set the example long before we talked about morning routines. He rose early, found quiet, and started the day with prayer. If it mattered to Him, it should matter to us.

But notice what else He did: He withdrew to prepare. Jesus wasn't just praying for Himself. He was strengthening Himself for the people He would encounter, the crowds He would teach, and the disciples He would lead. His solitude wasn't an escape; it was a strategy. It was intentional preparation for the responsibility ahead.

That's the essence of a morning routine. It builds you before the world needs you. It prepares you to lead with clarity instead of reacting with chaos. A routine is not about productivity. It is about stability. It grounds you before pressure ever has a chance to shake you. It determines how you show up when pressure inevitably arrives.

Chapter 1 was about deciding. Chapter 2 was about proving. This chapter is about removing the need to decide at all. It is about building a system that carries you automatically.

Mornings make or break you. If you don't fill your cup in the morning, chaos will knock you off balance fast. You'll react instead of respond. You'll lead with urgency instead of clarity.

I know this firsthand. Back when I had no routine, I rolled out of bed late, checked my phone before I even brushed my teeth, and walked into the day already behind. I was short-tempered and reactive. My business felt scattered, and so did I. I was starting every day on defense instead of leading it with intention.

When I committed to owning my mornings, everything shifted. I had focus, energy, and control before anyone else's demands could hit me. That's when I realized: a morning routine isn't optional. It's the foundation on which everything else is built. You do not rise to your goals. You fall to your routines.

A foundation is the part of a building you don't see, but everything else depends on it. If it's weak, the whole structure cracks under pressure. If it's strong, the building can stand through storms, weight, and time.

Your routine works the same way. Nobody else may see it. Nobody claps when you wake up early, pray, or do push-ups in the dark. But those unseen disciplines are what keep you standing when the pressures of business, leadership, and life hit you. They are what determine whether you stay steady or collapse under stress.

Jesus even used this imagery in Matthew 7 when He said the wise man built his house on the rock. The storm came for both the wise and the foolish, and the difference was what they had underneath them. That's why I call your routine a foundation. It's not flashy, but it's everything. It doesn't eliminate pressure, but it makes you unshakable when pressure comes.

Pressure will break you if you're not grounded. A morning routine is the anchor. It removes the need to decide again. When a decision is removed, the internal fight goes with it. You already made the decision. Your routine makes sure you follow through without thinking. On the days I skip mine, I feel it immediately: distracted mind, weak energy, short fuse. On the days I stay consistent, I'm sharper, calmer, and stronger. Same problems, different response.

Science backs this up. Neuroscientists call it *decision fatigue*: your brain only has so much willpower and clarity each day. Every decision drains it. A consistent routine reduces that drain. It automates the first part of your day, so you save your best energy for leadership, problem-solving, and creativity.

Routine is not restriction. It is freedom. It frees your mind to focus on what actually matters. What becomes automatic no longer requires discipline. And that is where real power begins.

University of Oklahoma psychologist Shawn McClean explains that routines act like shortcuts: when you accomplish tasks in the same order every morning, you conserve limited mental bandwidth for the high-level decisions leadership requires. Employees who complete their routine uninterrupted perform better and remain calmer. Those who start with disorder end the day mentally exhausted. The way you start your day directly impacts how you finish it.

Habits live in the basal ganglia, the brain's habit center. Repetition wires them into automatic behavior. That's why elite performers, from athletes to CEOs, guard their mornings so fiercely. They're not relying on willpower. They've built habits that run on autopilot.

For me, mornings always start the same way. The second my feet hit the floor, I bow my head and pray. That ritual anchors me before emails, calls, or problems rush in. Sometimes I pray again later in the sauna with the lights off. I talk to God about everything: the things I want, the things I fear, even the things I'd rather not admit. He already knows, but speaking it builds trust.

From there, I stack disciplines: wake up early, sweat, pray or read scripture, journal, cold plunge, and take vitamins. Each one serves a purpose, physical, mental, or spiritual alignment. I didn't start with all of these at once. I added them one by one until they became non-negotiable. The hardest? Cold plunges. Every part of my body wants comfort. But that's the point. Each plunge reminds me I can choose discipline when my body wants excuses.

The truth is, everyone already has a routine. It might be rolling out of bed, grabbing coffee, and scrolling your phone. That's still a routine. It just doesn't serve where you are trying to go. The question is whether your habits push you forward or hold you back.

This isn't just my story. It's how the greats operate. Navy SEAL commander Jocko Willink is famous for posting his 4:30 AM watch photo every morning. He says discipline in the morning gives him dominance over the rest of the day. Apple CEO Tim Cook starts his day at 3:45 AM to get clarity before the world wakes up. Tony Robbins begins each morning with breathwork, visualization, and movement to align his body and mind. Ed Mylett calls his approach "blissful dissatisfaction," beginning with gratitude and prayer before hitting his workout.

Different methods, same principle: if you win the morning, you win the day. Neuroscience confirms it. Morning routines that include movement and reflection boost dopamine and serotonin, which are tied to focus, motivation, and mood stability. That's why morning exercisers not only perform better but also handle stress more calmly throughout the day. By training your body early, you're training your brain to be resilient before challenges arrive.

Here's what my mornings look like today:

Larry's Morning Routine

- Wake up early (4:00 AM)
- Prayer (as soon as my feet hit the floor)
- Workout (60–90 minutes functional training: push-ups, pull-ups, weighted walks, or cardio)
- Scripture or journaling
- Cold plunge (3 minutes, 46–50 degrees)

- Vitamins and supplements
- Sauna or quiet reflection

I didn't start with all of these. I built them one by one. The cold plunge is still the hardest, but it's the one that reminds me daily that discipline is stronger than comfort.

My own story proves it, too. When I first committed to working out consistently, I could barely do 10 push-ups and 1 pull-up. Twenty-two months later, I can do 60–120 push-ups and 30–100 pull-ups every day. The difference wasn't motivation. It wasn't luck. It was routine. One habit stacked onto another until it became part of who I am.

Most people fail at routines because they try to do too much too fast. They try to overhaul everything at once, and when it doesn't stick, they quit. Discipline doesn't work like that. It's built in layers. Start small. Pick two habits that energize you. Do them every day for seven days. No skipping and no excuses. Track how you feel: your energy, your focus, your mood. Then add one more. Over time, your mornings become non-negotiable. Not because you have to, but because you've seen who you are when you do.

I tell people this all the time: keep it simple. If you can brush your teeth every morning, you can do 10 push-ups. You already have proof that you can be consistent, you just need to apply it intentionally.

You don't need a gym. You don't need an hour. Start with two minutes, five minutes, one glass of water, and one prayer. Anchor yourself in something positive instead of leaving it up to chance.

Your routine won't look exactly like mine, and it shouldn't. The best routine is the one you'll actually do. But it has to exist. Because how you start your day will decide how you show up for everything that follows.

****

Action Steps:

Build Your Routine

1. Pick two habits that give you energy and focus. Keep it simple. Not ten. Not five. Two. Simple works. Complex fails.
2. Commit for 7 days straight. No skipping. No excuses.
3. Track your results. Each night, ask: *Was I sharper? More focused? More calm?*
4. Do not judge the process. Just observe the outcome.
5. After 7 days, add one new habit. Build slowly, stack over time.
6. Protect your mornings. Treat them like oxygen: *non-negotiable.* If you lose your morning, you lose control of your day.

"Because of the Lord's great love we are not consumed, for his compassions never fail. They are new every morning; great is your faithfulness."

~Lamentations 3:22–23 (NIV)~

~Chapter 3 Workbook~

Build Your Routine System

This is where discipline becomes automatic. You are no longer deciding. You are no longer proving. You are building something that runs without thinking.

1. Your First Two Habits

What are the two habits you will start with?

2. Your Order

What order will you do them in? Routine is sequence. Sequence creates flow.

3. Time Block

What time will your routine start?

Time:

How long will it take?

---

4. Your Routine Plan

Write your exact routine step by step:

---

5. Keep It Real

Can you realistically do this every day?

YES ☐ NO ☐

If not, simplify it until it becomes undeniable.

6. 7-Day Consistency

Day 1 ☐
Day 2 ☐
Day 3 ☐
Day 4 ☐
Day 5 ☐
Day 6 ☐
Day 7 ☐

7. What Became Automatic

What started to feel easier or natural?

____

____

____

____

8. What Needs Adjustment

What felt forced or unrealistic?

9. Stack Your Next Habit

What is the next habit you will add?

Discipline builds it. Routine sustains it. What you repeat daily becomes who you are permanently.

"Trust in the Lord with all your heart and lean not on your own understanding; in all your ways submit to Him, and He will make your paths straight."
~Proverbs 3:5–6 (NIV)~

Routine is how you commit daily. Consistency is how it becomes established. Each morning reinforces the standard you are choosing to live by. God's mercies are new every morning, and so is your opportunity to lead with strength. When you own your morning, the rest of the day falls in line.

Next, we shift from what you are building to what you must remove. Because growth is not just about addition. It is also about elimination.

Chapter 4

Cut What Doesn't Serve You

"He cuts off every branch in me that bears no fruit while every branch that does bear fruit he prunes so that it will be even more fruitful."

~John 15:2 (NIV)~

Jesus made it clear about growth. It requires pruning. If you want to produce more fruit in your life, you have to cut what no longer serves you. Growth is not just about what you add. It is about what you are willing to remove. It is the discipline of elimination that creates space for real progress.

Most people think success comes from addition: more hours, more meetings, more strategies, more commitments. Hustle culture celebrates being busy as if activity equals progress. The truth is momentum often comes from subtraction and from removing what drains your focus, your energy, and your clarity.

Subtraction creates space. And space is what allows clarity to return.

I learned this the hard way. There was a time when my calendar was full, my days were packed, and yet I felt scattered. When I finally stepped back and looked at my calendar, my habits, and my relationships, I realized how much of my energy was being spent on things that produced no real return. I was busy but not always effective. Productive on paper but depleted in reality. I was moving constantly, but not always moving forward.

That moment taught me something important. You do not need more. You need less of what is holding you back. Growth is not always about doing more, it is about removing what is in the way.

We live in a culture that glorifies "more." Hustle culture tells us to stack commitments, fill every minute, add another tool, and say yes to every opportunity. But the more you add, the more diluted you become. Decision fatigue sets in. Clarity disappears. The more directions you move in, the less effective you become in any one of them.

Research backs this up. Studies from Yale University show that clutter, both physical and mental, limits the brain's ability to focus and process information. The same principle applies to your schedule and relationships. Too much noise kills clarity.

Leadership thinkers say the same thing. Greg McKeown, author of *Essentialism*, writes, *"If you don't prioritize your life, someone else will."*

If you do not control your time, someone else will fill it for you. Cutting is not weakness. It is wisdom. It is leadership over your time, your energy, and your direction.

One of the most powerful tools you can use is a life audit. Look at your week honestly and ask yourself where your time is leaking.

1. Who drains your energy instead of fueling it?
2. Which habits or commitments no longer align with your values?

When I did this, I saw how often being busy had replaced being intentional. Anyone can be busy. Not everyone is effective. Busy is not productive, and full is not the same as focused.

Learning to say no felt awkward at first. But over time, people adjusted. When you place a high value on your time, others do too. If you do not, they will take as much of it as you allow. Your boundaries teach people how to treat your time.

Some cuts are simple. Fewer meetings. Less screen time. Cleaner schedules. Other cuts are harder. Sometimes it is a toxic relationship. Sometimes it is a habit that once served you, but no longer does. Sometimes it is an opportunity that looks good but pulls you away from what actually matters. Not every opportunity is an assignment, and not every open door should be walked through.

Not everything that is good is right for you. Not everything that is available is aligned.

One of the hardest cuts I ever made came early in my life. Right after high school, I had two best friends I had grown up with. We were inseparable. But our paths started to diverge. I wanted more out of life. I wanted to build something meaningful. I knew if I stayed in that environment, I would never become the man I was called to be. Walking away was painful. At that age, it felt permanent. Looking back, it saved my future. It created the space I needed to grow into who I was meant to become.

Those decisions felt heavy at the time, but they created space for growth. I learned a principle that has stayed with me ever since. Every decision either moves you closer to your future or keeps you attached to your past. There is no neutral ground.

Like pruning a tree, the goal is not destruction. The goal is healthier growth. When you cut what does not serve you, you create room for what does. Less distraction brings more focus. Less clutter brings more clarity. Less toxicity brings more peace.

Research confirms this. When distractions are removed, the prefrontal cortex becomes more effective. That is the part of the brain responsible for decision-making and self-control. Subtraction strengthens leadership. Clarity improves when noise is removed.

As I made hard cuts over time, something shifted. My energy returned. My focus sharpened. I had more clarity at this stage of life than I ever had before. Clarity is not found by adding more. It is revealed when you remove what is in the way.

The process stayed the same even as my goals evolved. I began thinking beyond myself, toward the example I was setting and the legacy I wanted to leave. Inheritance is not just financial. It is wisdom. Discipline. Example. It is what people see modeled consistently over time.

As it says in Proverbs,

"A good man leaves an inheritance to his children's children, but the wealth of the sinner is stored up for the righteous."

~Proverbs 13:22 NIV~

As I look back over the decisions I have made, I still use the same filter today that I learned decades ago. Does this take me closer to my goal or farther away from it? The goals may change, but the process remains the same.

That lens reshaped how I live now. I am more focused at sixty-two than I was at any point in my life earlier. I have more energy. More clarity. More intention. Not because I added more, but because I cut what did not serve the future I wanted to leave behind.

What drives me now is not just success, but stewardship. I want to leave my children and my grandchildren more than resources. I want to leave them an example. I want them to see discipline lived out, not just talked about.

Pruning made that possible.

When you cut what does not align, you do not lose yourself. You refine yourself. You create space for the life you are meant to pass forward. You become more focused, not less capable.

Addition without intention leads to burnout. Subtraction with clarity leads to growth.

****

Action Steps:
Cut What Doesn't Serve You

1. **Audit your week.** Write down where your time, energy, and focus go. What gets measured gets visible.

2. **Identify the drains.** Which habits, commitments, or relationships leave you depleted?

3. **Cut one for 30 days.** Don't try to eliminate everything at once. Choose one and commit to removing it. One clean cut is more powerful than ten weak attempts.

4. **Notice the shift.** Track what changes: your focus, your energy, your clarity. Pay attention to what improves when the distraction is gone.

"I have the right to do anything," you say, "but not everything is beneficial. I have the right to do anything, but not everything is constructive."

~1 Corinthians 10:23 NIV~

Paul reminds us that not everything available to us is actually good for us.

The things you cut will shape you just as much as the things you add. If you want to grow, prune. If you want clarity, subtract. If you want momentum, cut what doesn't serve you.

~Chapter 4 Workbook~

Cut What Doesn't Serve You
Your Elimination Audit

Remove what is in the way. You are clearing space so growth can happen.

1. Where Your Time Goes

List your typical day or week:

____

____

____

____

2. Energy Drains

What leaves you feeling depleted, distracted, or off track?

____

____

____

3. Misaligned Commitments

What are you saying yes to that does not align with your goals?

---

4. The One Cut

What is ONE thing you will eliminate or reduce for the next 30 days?

---

5. Why It Needs to Go

What is this costing you?

---

6. Replacement

What will you do instead with that time or energy?

____

____

7. 30-Day Commitment

I commit to removing this for 30 days:

YES ☐ NO ☐

8. What Changed

After removing it, what improved?

Focus:

____

____

Energy:

____

____

Clarity:

____

____

What you remove matters just as much as what you build.

"Let us throw off everything that hinders and the sin that so easily entangles."
~Hebrews 12:1 NIV~

You cannot run forward while holding onto what is slowing you down. Forward movement requires letting go. Next, we shift from what you remove to what fuels you. Because once you clear the space, you must fill it with the right energy.

Chapter 5
Fuel Your Body.
Clear Your Head.

"Do you not know that your bodies are temples of the Holy Spirit, who is in you, whom you have received from God? You are not your own; you were bought at a price. Therefore, honor God with your bodies."

~1 Corinthians 6:19-20 (NIV)~

God created our bodies as vessels not just to survive, but to serve. If you want to think clearly, lead strongly, and live with purpose, you have to fuel the vessel. Most entrepreneurs try to out-grind exhaustion. They live on caffeine, skip meals, and promise to rest "after the launch." They treat energy as optional when it is actually foundational.

Burnout is not a badge of honor. It is a warning signal. When your body breaks down, your leadership follows. When your energy drops, your decision-making, patience, and clarity drop with it.

I learned that firsthand. In 2018, during triathlon training, a heart test revealed blockage in my Widowmaker artery. It shook me. For a while, I spiraled, and then a friend said, *"Maybe God's not done with you yet."*

That moment forced me to reevaluate how I was treating the very thing that carries everything I am responsible for, and that changed everything. Your body is not something you own. It is something you are entrusted with. Our bodies aren't our property; they're on loan from Him. They have been entrusted to you for a purpose. How we treat them determines how long and how well we can carry the responsibility placed on us.

Here is the lesson for you. Energy is not optional. It is your competitive advantage. Without it, you are grinding through mental fog. With it, you operate with clarity, confidence, and control. Ask yourself honestly: *Are you treating your body like a business asset or like an afterthought?* From that day, I began stewarding mine with the same discipline I brought to business.

Your body is your operating system. Garbage in produces garbage out. Clean fuel produces clean focus. What you consume directly impacts how you think, decide, and lead.

Harvard research shows that refined sugar and processed foods cloud memory and slow decision-making, while clean, whole foods sharpen focus and regulate mood. Sleep deprivation impairs judgment as much as alcohol. The quality of your inputs determines the quality of your leadership.

Peak performance isn't hustle. It's stewardship. Food is not just comfort, it is chemistry that affects how your brain performs. When you eat for performance, your brain performs.

When I cut sugar entirely, the difference was immediate. Sharper focus, steadier mood, more energy. Clarity is not something you chase. It is something you create through discipline. It is the result of consistent inputs, not occasional effort. I stopped guessing and started measuring. Bloodwork, hydration, nutrient timing, and sleep quality. Once you realize how much control you actually have, you stop winging it and start leading yourself like a professional athlete.

Do the same. You do not need to overhaul everything at once. Start small. Cut one processed food for seven days. Drink more water. Add one quality protein source and greens. Pay attention to what happens to your patience, your clarity, and your ability to think under pressure. Every input is either fueling you or draining you. There is no neutral. The goal isn't perfection, it's progress you can feel. Every bite is either building you up or breaking you down.

Fuel is more than food. It is how you move, how you rest, and how you recover. Movement is essential. The body was designed to move, and movement directly increases neuroplasticity. That is the brain's ability to learn, adapt, and regulate emotion. Even simple movement like a short walk lowers stress hormones and improves your ability to think clearly.

Sleep is not optional. I used to brag about functioning on five hours until I actually tracked my sleep and realized I had been operating in chronic deprivation for years. Now I strive for seven hours minimum. You may be surviving on less sleep, but you are not performing at your full capacity. Imagine who you would be when you were fully charged.

Recovery is not weakness. It is how you reload the system. Cold plunges, saunas, stretching, and silence. These practices reset your nervous system so you can show up again tomorrow with clarity. Choose one recovery ritual and treat it like a non-negotiable meeting with yourself.

There is a reason elite performers train their bodies as intentionally as their businesses. When you control your body, you prove to your brain that feelings do not run you. Principles do. I don't jump into freezing water each morning because it's fun. I do it because it trains my nervous system to do hard things on command. It reinforces that I act based on commitment, not comfort.

Discipline in the body creates discipline in the mind. Once you conquer discomfort early in the day, the frustrations of traffic, email, and conflict don't rattle you. You've already won the hardest battle of the day. Everything else becomes easier to handle by comparison.

That's what Jocko Willink means when he says, "Discipline equals freedom." Freedom from mood. Freedom from excuses. Freedom to lead without being reactive. When you build discipline in your body, it carries into your leadership. People sense it before you speak. Your steadiness creates trust. You don't have to talk about your work ethic. They feel it in your presence. Consistency is visible before it is ever spoken.

Ask yourself: *If my body language is the first message I send, what story am I telling?*

****

Action Steps:

Fuel Your Body.

Clear Your Head.

1. **Audit your fuel.** Track everything you eat and drink for three days. Notice what gives energy and what drains it.
2. **Move daily.** Choose one practice: walking, stretching, lifting, or training, and make it non-negotiable.
3. **Protect your sleep.** Aim for seven hours or more with consistent bed and wake times.
4. **Recover deliberately.** Add one recovery ritual, such as cold exposure, heat, silence, or journaling.
5. **Cut one toxin for 7 days.** Sugar, alcohol, or processed food. Observe the difference in your clarity, focus, and energy.

*"So whether you eat or drink or whatever you do, do it
all for the glory of God."*
~1 Corinthians 10:31 (NIV)~

Fueling your body is not vanity. It is worship. It is the stewardship of the vessel God entrusted to you. When you treat it with honor, your clarity improves, your leadership sharpens, and your impact multiplies. Your body is not separate from your business. It is your business. Fuel it well. Think clearly. Lead boldly.

~Chapter 5 Workbook~

Fuel and Focus Reset

This is not about perfection. This is about awareness and control.

1. Your Current Fuel Reality

What did you eat and drink over the last 3 days?

Day 1 :

____

Day 2 :

____

Day 3 :

____

2. Energy Check

After eating, how did you feel? Focused or foggy? Energized or tired?

____

____

3. Your Biggest Drain

What is the ONE thing that is hurting your energy the most?

____

____

____

4. Your 7 Day Cut

What will you remove for the next 7 days?

____

____

____

5. Movement Commitment

What is your daily movement habit? (Example: Walk 20 minutes after lunch, Strength train for 30 minutes, no phone) Be specific:

____

____

____

6. Sleep Standard

What time will you go to bed? What time will you wake up?

7. Recovery Practice

Choose ONE:

- ☐ Cold exposure
- ☐ Sauna or heat
- ☐ Stretching
- ☐ Silence or prayer

Time committed:

8. Results After 7 Days

Focus:

Energy:

____

____

Mood:

____

____

You cannot think clearly in a body that is running on empty.

"I discipline my body and keep it under control..."
~ 1 Corinthians 9:27 (ESV)~

Fueling your body is not vanity. It is worship. It is stewardship of the vessel God entrusted to you. When you treat it with honor, your clarity improves, your leadership sharpens, and your impact multiplies.

Your body is not separate from your business. It is the foundation of it.

Chapter 6
Lead from the Inside Out

"Above all else, guard your heart, for everything you do flows from it."

~Proverbs 4:23 (NIV)~

Leadership does not start with what's on the outside: a title, a role, the corner office, or authority. It starts inside. Before you lead people, you lead yourself first. If your heart, your values, and your integrity are not anchored, nothing you build will last. You can scale a business without character, but you cannot sustain it. Eventually, what is inside you will leak out into how you lead. Leadership is always revealed over time, not just in moments of success, but in moments of pressure.

Every decision, every reaction, every conversation flows from what is happening beneath the surface. That is why Scripture tells us to guard the heart first. Not the calendar. Not the strategy. The heart.

I have led from two very different places in my life. One was ego. The other was principle. The outcomes could not have been more different.

When I led from ego, I was reactive and burned out. I pushed people too hard. I measured myself through control and authority. I made decisions out of frustration instead of clarity. The results came fast, but they did not last. Trust eroded. Relationships strained. I carried constant pressure because everything depended on me being right. Everything felt heavier because I was trying to control what should have been led.

When I shifted to leading from principle, something changed. I did not need to force alignment. People followed because they trusted me. Decisions became clearer. Pressure lifted. Leadership became steadier, not louder. Ego demands control, while principle earns trust. That is the difference between managing behavior and leading hearts.

There was a moment years ago that made this painfully clear to me. I was under immense pressure in business and got into a heated argument with one of my most loyal employees. She had been with me for years and had carried the business through difficult times. In frustration, I said something I should never have said. I reminded her that I signed her paycheck.

At the time, it felt like a throwaway comment. It was not. When I saw her days later, she was distant. When I asked what was wrong, she told me exactly what I had said and how deeply it hurt her. She was emotional. I was ashamed. That moment exposed something in me. Ego had spoken. Not leadership. It revealed a gap between who I thought I was as a leader and how I was actually showing up.

I apologized. I hugged her. I told her I would never speak that way again. And I meant it. That experience stayed with me because it reminded me of this truth.

Confidence is not the same as arrogance. Authority is not the same as dominance. Leadership is not proven by reminding people who is in charge. It is proven by how safe people feel under your leadership. It is proven by the trust you create, not the control you demand.

True leadership does not come from pressure or position. It comes from alignment. Psychology supports this. Research on ego-driven leadership consistently shows that leaders who operate from pride and insecurity may produce short-term results, but they destroy long-term trust. The ego is fragile and reactive. Leaders who operate from ego need constant validation, and when they don't get it, they crack. Teams led by ego experience higher turnover, lower engagement, and more conflict.

The ego needs validation. Principle provides stability. Ego is emotional and reacts. Principle is anchored and responds.

Principle-led leadership is different. It's steady. It's strong. It's sustainable. When you're aligned with your core values, your decisions have clarity. Even when people disagree, they respect the consistency and clarity behind your decisions.

That is why I built my leadership around a simple code, Do What's Right ™· It is written everywhere as a reminder. Doing what is right is not always easy. It is often costly. But it is always right.

For me, that code is *Do What's Right™*. It's the framework:

Decision. Discipline. Determination. Deliver.

Early in my career, I learned this lesson the hard way. I underbid a job so badly that it was going to cost me money to complete the job. I knew it. The client knew it. I could have walked away but at the time, I had no money. Walking away would have saved me ten thousand dollars I did not have. But I had given my word. So I did the job and absorbed the loss. That customer is still with me more than twenty five years later. That decision defined how I would lead moving forward.

Principle cost me in the moment. Integrity paid me over decades. That is how it works. Ego looks for immediate relief. Principle looks for lasting impact.

Every strong leader lives by a personal code. It does not need to be public, but it must be clear. It becomes your filter when emotions are high and stakes are heavy. Without a code, you'll always drift. With one, you decide faster, lead steadier, and always have direction.

Ask yourself these questions honestly:

- What do I stand for when no one is watching?
- What will I not compromise no matter the cost?
- What principles guide my decisions when pressure hits?

Much of my own code came from mentors, both good and bad. I learned just as much from people who showed me what not to do as from those who modeled excellence. Both shaped how I lead today.

One of the earliest influences on me was a business owner named Alec Beck. He ran his company with absolute clarity around integrity. He believed trust was non negotiable. He would fire someone over something as small as stealing a pencil.

At the time, I thought it was extreme. Later, I understood. He was setting a standard. Standards create clarity, and clarity eliminates hesitation.

When standards are clear, decisions are easy. There is no debate or gray area. You simply do what is right. That example stayed with me long after he passed. It shaped how I lead today.

Action Steps:

Lead from the Inside Out

1. Write your personal leadership code. Keep it simple. Three to five principles. Clarity creates consistency. Consistency reinforces identity.
2. Share it with your family or your team. Accountability strengthens integrity.
3. Test every decision against it for the next thirty days.
4. Notice how clarity increases when your actions align with your values. When your code is clear, your decisions become faster and stronger.

Scripture reinforces this principle:

"The integrity of the upright guides them, but the unfaithful are destroyed by their duplicity."

~Proverbs 11:3 NIV~

Integrity guides. Ego destroys. Principle sustains. Leading from the inside out means your values drive your actions, not your emotions. It means you choose consistency over convenience. It means your leadership does not change depending on who is in the room or what is at stake. When you lead this way, something powerful happens. People trust you. Not because you demand it, but because your behavior consistently proves it. Your presence becomes steady. Your decisions become clear. Even when people disagree, they respect your consistently because they know where you stand.

Integrity is the anchor of leadership. Without it, authority collapses under pressure. With it, you do not need titles, control, or force. Your character speaks for you before you ever open your mouth. The strongest leaders do not push harder. They stand firmer. They lead from alignment, not impulse. From principle, not pride. Leadership is not built from the outside in. It is built from the inside out. When your heart is aligned, your leadership becomes clear. Not easy, but consistent and unwavering.

That is the shift. Lead from the inside out.

~Chapter 6 Workbook~

Build Your Leadership Code

This is where leadership becomes real.
Not what you say. What you live.

1. Your Core Values

What do you truly stand for?

____

____

____

____

2. Non Negotiables

What will you NOT compromise, no matter the situation?

____

____

____

3. Your Leadership Code

Write 3 to 5 clear principles you will live by:

1. ____

2. ____

3. ____

4. ____

5. ____

4. Pressure Test

Think of a recent tough situation. Did you lead from ego or principle?

____

____

____

5. Rewrite the Response

How would you respond differently using your code?

____

____

____

6. Daily Filter

Before your next big decision, ask: Does this align with my code?

YES ☐ NO ☐

7. 30-Day Alignment

Track one decision per day where you consciously chose principle over reaction:

____

____

____

____

"Whoever walks in integrity walks securely, but whoever takes crooked paths will be found out."

~Proverbs 10:9 (NIV)~

Integrity is not something you turn on. It is something you live from. Now comes the final test. Execution. Consistency. Follow through. Next, we bring everything together.

Deliver. Every single day.

Chapter 7
Deliver. Every Darn Day

"Whatever you do, work at it with all your heart, as working for the Lord, not for human masters."

~Colossians 3:23 (NIV)~

Excellence is not built in one defining moment. It is built on the quiet decision to show up with discipline day after day, even when no one is watching. Most people only count the big wins. They obsess over what they have not done yet, what goals they missed, or what someone else is achieving. But confidence is not built in leaps. It is built through repetition, one layer at a time. It is built through consistent delivery, not occasional intensity.

I learned this over time through something most people would not expect. When people ask me what my greatest success has been, they usually assume it is money, growth, or scale. It is none of those.

My greatest success is that I still have employees working with me today who I hired more than twenty-five years ago, and I have retired several in just the last two years. That did not happen by accident. It happened because of daily delivery. Showing up. Making hard calls. Standing by people when things were difficult. Staying consistent when it would have been easier to walk away. That level of consistency builds something most people overlook, trust over time.

Consistency built trust. Trust built longevity. Those kinds of wins do not make headlines. But they compound. And what compounds becomes sustainable.

Over time, those small daily decisions rewired how I saw myself. I stopped being someone who tried. I became someone who delivers.

Science backs this up. The brain is wired to respond to progress. Each time you complete a task or acknowledge a win, your brain releases dopamine. That chemical reinforces confidence, resilience, and motivation. Progress is proof, and proof builds identity.

It tells your nervous system, I am capable. I am moving forward. This creates a positive feedback loop. The more progress you recognize, the more momentum you build. This is why small wins prevent burnout and sustain performance over long periods of time.

Breakthroughs are built on small, consistent actions. Every time you acknowledge a small win, you reinforce progress. Every time you ignore one, you fuel discouragement and stress. This is not just motivational language. It is how the brain works.

Tracking those wins makes the effect even stronger. Research shows that people who physically write down or check off their progress, whether it is workouts, business habits, or daily disciplines, are far more consistent over time. Seeing proof on paper matters. It gives your brain evidence. And evidence changes identity. You stop saying, *"I hope I can."* You start saying, *"This is who I am."*

The opposite is also true. When progress goes unnoticed, stress hormones like cortisol rise. You feel behind even when you are not. That pressure erodes confidence and leads people to quit early. The problem is often not failure, it is unrecognized progress. People are not tracking what they are actually doing right.

That lesson matters deeply in entrepreneurship. This journey is not for the faint of heart. Roughly half of businesses fail in the first five years, and most of the rest do not survive the next five. Setbacks are not the exception. They are the rule. Everyone sees you when you are on the peak, but they do not see the valleys. You are either coming out of one or heading into one.

The peak is narrow for a reason. You are not meant to live there. You pass through it. The ones who last are not the ones who avoid difficulty, but the ones who keep delivering through it.

Great baseball players fail seven out of ten times. Entrepreneurs fail closer to nine out of ten. The difference between those who last and those who quit is resilience. Not just mental. Physical, emotional, and spiritual.

That is why small wins matter. Maybe you closed a deal today. Maybe you made the call you were avoiding. Maybe you kept a promise to yourself when no one else was watching. Those wins stack. They build something bigger than momentum. They build self trust which becomes the foundation for every future decision you make.

There is a cost when you do not deliver. When you fail to follow through, people stop trusting you. Opportunities disappear. Credibility erodes. And it is not just external. You stop trusting yourself.

No matter what business you are in, you are in the service business. You may sell products, expertise, leadership, or ideas, but what people actually experience is whether you follow through. In my world, that means manufacturing roof and floor systems on strict timelines. When we miss, entire projects stall. Crews wait. Costs pile up. Trust erodes.

That pressure taught me something early. Delivery is not optional. It is not a skill you turn on when it is convenient. It is part of your identity. It is something people come to expect from you. When people know you deliver, they relax. When they trust you to follow through, opportunities expand. And when you fail to deliver, even once, it leaves a mark.

Delivering isn't just for business. It belongs in every arena of your life. Deliver in your body by taking care of your health. Deliver in your faith by showing up for God daily. Deliver in your family by being present and dependable. Deliver in your business by keeping promises, big or small. Consistency across these areas creates integrity in your life. How you do one thing is how you do everything.

Every time you keep a promise to yourself, you strengthen your identity. Every time you break one, you weaken it. When you constantly feel behind, your body produces stress hormones that keep you anxious and reactive. When you notice progress, you interrupt that cycle. Instead of feeling stuck, you begin to feel steady.

Motivation may get you started, but discipline is what keeps you growing. And delivery is what proves it.

There will always be someone with a bigger company, a faster trajectory, or a louder platform. Comparison will always leave you feeling behind. Consistency is what moves you forward.

The only scoreboard that matters is your own. Delivering daily is not just about today. It prepares you for tomorrow. Every small win compounds. Every act of discipline positions you for opportunities you cannot see yet. Not delivering is rarely about one broken promise. It is about the slow erosion of trust both with others and within yourself.

Psychologists call this behavioral integrity. People trust leaders whose actions consistently match their words. When your delivery is consistent, people know they can rely on you, and when they can rely on you, they will follow you. This is not just about business. It applies everywhere in your life.

Small things are never small. They are training grounds for the person you are becoming. Scripture makes this clear:

"Whoever can be trusted with very little can also be trusted with much."
~Luke 16:10 (NIV) ~

So what does this look like in practice?

Winning the day does not require perfection. It requires intention and clarity. Define what a win looks like before the day starts. Keep it simple. Three priorities at most. Track at least one win each day for the next two weeks. Write it down. Review it. Stop measuring yourself against someone else's pace.

When you deliver in the small things, you prepare yourself for greater responsibility. At the end of each week, look back and ask yourself one honest question. Did I deliver on what mattered?

"Let us not become weary in doing good, for at the proper time we will reap a harvest if we do not give up."
~Galatians 6:9 (NIV)~

The harvest does not come from one day of effort. It comes from steady, disciplined delivery. Don't give up Keep showing up. You do not have to go big every day. You have to act with intention. Deliver. Every darn day. Because in the end, it is not about what you said. It is about what you actually did. Execution is what builds identity. That is how momentum becomes unstoppable.

****

Action Steps:

Deliver. Every Darn Day.

1. **Define your win.** Write down the top three things that would make tomorrow a win. No more than three. If everything else falls apart, these are the non-negotiables.
2. **Track daily progress.** For the next 14 days, record at least one win each day. Write it down where you can see it *(journal, whiteboard, or phone note).*
3. **Acknowledge the small victories.** Don't brush them off. Celebrate the reps, the calls, the workouts, the moments you showed up. They count more than you think.
4. **Resist comparison.** Each night, ask yourself: *Did I deliver on my wins?* Not "Did I beat someone else?"

Review weekly. At the end of two weeks, look back at your list. Notice how the small wins have stacked. Pay attention to the confidence you've built.

~Chapter 7 Workbook~

The 14 Day Delivery Challenge

This is where identity is proven. Not in what you plan, but in what you execute.

1. Your Top 3 Daily Wins

1. ____

2. ____

3. ____

2. 14-Day Win Tracker

Day 1:

____

____

Day 2:

____

____

Day 3:

____

____

Day 4:

____

____

Day 5:

____

____

Day 6:

____

____

Day 7:

Day 8:

Day 9:

Day 10:

Day 11:

Day 12:

____

____

Day 13:

____

____

Day 14:

____

____

3. Self Trust Check

Did you follow through?

YES ☐ NO ☐

4. Identity Shift

After 14 days, who have you proven yourself to be?

____

____

5. Your Standard

I am someone who:

____

____

____

____

"Well done, good and faithful servant."
~Matthew 25:23 (NIV)~

Faithfulness is proven in consistency. Not once. Every day. Consistency is what separates intention from identity. Now we bring everything together, not as ideas, but as a code.

Next: The Do What's Right™ Code

Chapter 8
The Do What's Right™ Code

"To do what is right and just is more acceptable to the Lord than sacrifice."

~ Proverbs 21:3 ~

When I look back at my journey, the wins, the losses, the setbacks, the comebacks, one thing rises above everything else. What made the difference was not talent. It was not timing. It was not luck. It was consistency in one standard.

It was a code.

For me, that code is simple and uncompromising. Do What's Right™.

A simple standard applied consistently over time. This code has guided how I lead my family, how I run my businesses, and how I make decisions when the pressure is high and the answers are unclear. It has carried me through moments where doing what was easy would have cost me everything that mattered. It became the filter I run everything through.

The truth is, I didn't always live by it. I've made choices I'm not proud of. I've cut corners, made decisions out of ego, and tried to force my own way. Every time I stepped outside the code, I paid the price. And every time I came back to it, I found strength, clarity, and alignment again. The results were always consistent, whether I followed it or ignored it.

Doing what's right isn't always the easiest or fastest path. It is rarely the most comfortable one, but it is always the right choice in the long term. It is the only path that builds something that lasts. Trust. Integrity. Respect. Peace. It's what grounds you when pressure rises and temptation calls.

The seven shifts you've walked through are how this code is lived out in real life. Decide before you feel ready. Refuse to chase motivation. Own your routine. Cut what doesn't serve you. Fuel your body and your mind. Lead from the inside out. Deliver every single day. Each one reinforces the same standard.

Decision. Discipline. Determination. Deliver.

- You decide before you feel ready.
- You discipline yourself when motivation fades.
- You stay determined when setbacks hit.
- You deliver when no one is watching.

Each shift is simply a different expression of the same truth. Do what is right, even when it costs you in the short term, because it always pays off in the long term.

There have been moments in my life where the choice was clear but difficult. Walk away from something profitable because it violates my standards. Take responsibility when it would have been easier to shift blame. Admit fault when pride wanted silence. Each of those moments shaped the man I became far more than any success ever did. The difficult decisions defined me more than the easy wins ever could.

Living by a code changes who you are at your core. You stop drifting and start making decisions with intention. You no longer chase every opportunity that comes your way. Instead, you create and choose opportunities that align with who you are and what you stand for. You move from reacting to leading, from uncertainty to conviction.

Scripture says:

"The Lord detests lying lips, but he delights in people who are trustworthy."

~Proverbs 12:22 (NIV)~

Trustworthiness is not built in a moment. It is built through consistent alignment between what you say and what you do. That is what a code creates. It becomes a filter for every decision, every partnership, and every temptation you face. If it does not align, you walk away without hesitation. If it does align, you move forward with clarity and confidence, knowing you are operating from principle, not impulse.

Here's the challenge: don't just read this book and nod along. Choose your code. Write it down. Live by it. Let it become the anchor that shapes your decisions and your direction. You don't need to adopt mine, but you need one of your own. Without it, you'll drift. With it, you'll stand strong.

At the end of the day, life and leadership are not about perfection. They're about principle. You won't always get it right. But if you commit to doing what's right, consistently, the results will take care of themselves. Consistency matters more than perfection.

This is how identity is built through consistent action over time.

****

Action Steps: The Do What's Right™ Code

1. **Write your code.** Take 10 minutes and put it on paper. Keep it short. You don't need more than one sentence, but make it clear enough to guide your life and leadership.
2. **Share it.** Tell someone you trust whether it be a spouse, a business partner, your team, etc, and invite them to hold you accountable.
3. **Test it.** For the next 30 days, run every decision you make through your code. If it doesn't align, cut it. If it does, commit to it.
4. **Live it.** Don't just talk about your code. Let people see it in your choices, your leadership, and your character.

If you've made it this far, I want you to hear me clearly: this is your moment.

You don't need another motivational speech. You don't need the perfect plan. You don't need to wait until you feel ready. You have everything you need right now to start building the life and leadership you've been called to.

The 7 Shifts aren't theory. They're the choices that rebuilt my life. They're the proof that discipline beats motivation, that clarity beats chaos, and that integrity beats ego. And now they're yours.

Nothing changes unless you act. Nothing shifts unless you decide. The people who live with purpose aren't the ones who talk about it, they are the ones who follow through.

So I'm leaving you with this: **Do What's Right**™. In business. In life. In you. Every decision, every day. Not because it is easy or comfortable, but because it produces fruit that lasts.

You are not born with it. You build it. And you build it through consistent action over time. And you can with one decision, one discipline, one day at a time. That is how identity is formed.

The future doesn't belong to the people who wait. It belongs to the people who act. So go and deliver, every single day.

~Chapter 8 Workbook~

The Do What's Right™ Code

This is not about doing more.

This is about defining who you are and living it consistently.

1. What Does *"Right"* Mean to You

What does *"Do What's Right™"* actually look like in your life, not in theory, but in practice? Think about the standards you refuse to compromise, even when it's hard, uncomfortable, or costly.

List the values that define your version of *"right"*:

____

____

____

____

____

____

2. Define Your Code

Write your personal code. Keep it clear and simple. One sentence.

I commit to: _______________________________

____

____

3. Where Have You Been Out of Alignment

This is where growth starts. Where have you recently not done what you knew was right? What did it cost you?

____

____

____

____

4. Your Non Negotiables

These are standards you will not break, no matter the situation.

____

____

____

5. Decision Filter

Before making a decision, run it through your code. Does this align with who you say you are?

YES ☐   NO ☐

If no, what needs to change?

6. 30-Day Code Commitment

For the next 30 days, I commit to living by this code in:

My business: ______________________________________

My family: ____

My health: ____

My faith: ____

Other: ____

7. Accountability

Who will hold you to your code?

Name: ____

How they will hold you accountable:

____

8. Identity Statement

Who are you choosing to become?

I am someone who: ___________________________

____

____

____

____

____

____

*"But be doers of the word, and not hearers only,
deceiving yourselves."*

~ James 1:22 (ESV) ~

Your code is your guard. Live it, and everything will follow.

Chapter 9
Epilogue: Built Not Born

What Comes Next

"Being confident of this, that He who began a good work in you will carry it on to completion until the day of Christ Jesus."
Philippians 1:6 (NIV)

When I started this journey, I didn't know how many walls I'd hit, how many times I'd fall flat, or how many times I'd have to rebuild. What I've learned is that being an entrepreneur, a leader, and a man of faith isn't about perfection. It's about persistence. It is about continuing to move forward, even when progress feels slow, uncertain, or difficult.

You've just walked through the 7 Shifts that rebuilt me, and I believe they can do the same for you. This book is not the finish line. It is the starting point for what comes next.

That's why I started the *Born or Made* Podcast. It's why I mentor entrepreneurs and leaders. And it's why I keep writing, speaking, and sharing. Not because I have all the answers, but because I have lived through the process of building, failing, learning, and rebuilding again.

If this book spoke to you, I invite you to keep walking with me. Subscribe to the podcast. Connect with me online. Share your story. Continue the work you have started here and build something that lasts.

Because at the end of the day, this isn't just about my journey. It's about yours. It is about the decisions you make, the standards you choose, and the life you are willing to build from this point forward.

"Therefore encourage one another and build each other up, just as in fact you are doing."

~ 1 Thessalonians 5:11 (NIV)~

What you have learned only matters if it is applied.

The question now is simple and direct:

What will you do next?

Decide. Then move.

Scripture Index

Chapter 1: Decide Before You're Ready
Proverbs 16:3
Matthew 5:37
James 4:17

Chapter 2: Stop Chasing Motivation
Hebrews 12:11
James 1:2–4
Proverbs 25:28
2 Timothy 4:7

Chapter 3: Your Routine is Your Foundation
Mark 1:35
Lamentations 3:22–23
Proverbs 3:5–6

Chapter 4: Cut What Doesn't Serve You
John 15:2
Proverbs 13:22
1 Corinthians 10:23
Hebrews 12:1

Chapter 5: Fuel Your Body. Clear Your Head.
1 Corinthians 6:19–20
1 Corinthians 10:31
1 Corinthians 9:27

Chapter 6: Lead From the Inside Out
Proverbs 4:23
Proverbs 11:3
Proverbs 10:9

Chapter 7: Deliver. Every Darn Day
Colossians 3:23
Luke 16:10
Galatians 6:9
Matthew 25:23

Chapter 8: The Do What's Right™ Code
Proverbs 21:3
Proverbs 12:22
James 1:22

Chapter 9: Epilogue
Philippians 1:6
1 Thessalonians 5:11

ACKNOWLEDGMENTS

This book didn't come to life alone. It's the product of the people who believed in me, challenged me, and pushed me to keep building when it would have been easier to quit.

To my family, thank you for your patience, your encouragement, and your constant reminders of what really matters. You've been my anchor in every season.

To my APEX team, thank you for living out *Do What's Right*™ alongside me every day. Your dedication and loyalty are proof that we are built, not born.

To my mentors and friends, those who spoke hard truths, lifted me in low times, and showed me the power of perseverance, I am forever grateful.

To Bridgetta Tomarchio of Plot Twist Ink, my co-author and partner in this project. Your gift for pulling stories out of me, shaping words, and keeping this book aligned with my voice and vision has been invaluable. This book wouldn't exist without your collaboration.

To the readers, listeners, and entrepreneurs who follow the *Born or Made* journey, this book is for you. Every story you've shared, every question you've asked, every time you've tuned in or reached out has fueled me to keep going.

And most of all, to the Lord, who gave me the strength and grace to get back up every time I fell. Without Him, none of this would matter.

ABOUT THE AUTHOR

Larry G. Dix II is a bestselling author, entrepreneur, and mentor who has built businesses, led teams, and rebuilt himself through discipline and faith. From his early days working in the lumberyards to founding APEX, Larry has lived the grind of leadership and learned what it takes to rise above setbacks.

As host of the *Born or Made Podcast,* he has interviewed hundreds of top entrepreneurs and leaders, exploring the question of whether greatness is innate or built. His life and work prove the answer: it's built.

When he's not leading in business, Larry is a cattle rancher, real estate investor, marathon runner, and devoted family man. He is passionate about mentoring entrepreneurs and executives to scale with structure, discipline, and purpose, guided by his life code: **Do What's Right™ — in business, in life, in you.**

https://www.larrygdix.com/